The CHEMAINUS MURALS

Festival of Murals

SINCE 1982

A Sincere Welcome

When you visit Chemainus, you are not only considered a Tourist, but we welcome you as our special guest and are proud to share our heritage and our community with you. Each Mural is identified by a number which corresponds with the photographs and stories in this book. You can find all the Murals by following the yellow footsteps on the sidewalks.

Enjoy your stay,

Virginia Blatchford.

Hanni Unruh

Cyrni Forbe

シュメイナスへようこそ！

一同、心より歓迎いたします。ここシュメイナスでは、あなたは只の旅行者ではなく、特別なお客様です。私たち自慢の壁画の町をごゆっくりご覧下さいませ。壁画には、それぞれ番号が付いていますので、この本の中の写真と解説をご参照いただくのにご利用ください。歩道の黄色い足跡をたどれば、すべての壁画をご覧になれます。

Soyez les Bienvenus

Lorsque vous visitez Chemainus, vous êtes non seulement traité comme un(e) tourist, mais aussi comme notre invité spécial. Nous sommes fier de partager avec vous notre heritage et notre communauté. Chaque peinture murale est identifiée par un numéro qui correspond aux photos et aux histoires de ce livre. Vous pouvez trouver toutes ces peintures murales en suivant les pas jaunes sur les trottoirs de Chemainus.

Amusez-vous bien!

Diane Doucet

¡Nuestra sincera bienvenida!

Cuando Ud visita Chemainus, le recibimos no solamente como turista sino también como huesped estimado. Nos da orgullo compartir nuestra herencia historica y nuestra comunidad. Cada pintura mural esta identificada con un numero que corresponde con las fotografías y cuentos en este libro. Encontrará cada obra siguiendo las huellas amarillas en la acera.

¡Qué disfrute su día!

Juanita M Haddad

Herzlich Willkommen

Wenn Sie nach Chemainus kommen sind Sie für uns mehr als ein Tourist, nämlich ein ganz spezieller Gast. Wir möchten Sie teilhaben lassen an unserer Geschichte und am Leben unserer Gemeinde, auf die wir sehr stolz sind. Jedes einzelne Wandgemälde hat eine Nummer, die mit den jeweiligen Photographien und Geschichten in diesem Buch übereinstimmt. Die Wandmalereien sind leicht zu finden. Man braucht nur den gelben Fuss-spuren auf den Gehwegen zu folgen.

Viel vergnügen

snume hlple

ברוכים הבאים

שלום מבקר יקר. בבקורך בשמאינס אינך נחשב לתייר בלבד אלא אורח מיוחד שאנו גאים לשתף בהיסטוריה ובחיי צירתינו המיוחדת. כל אחד ואחד מציורי הקיר המיוחדים ממוספר ותאם למספר ולפרטי הסיפור בספר זה. אתה יכול למצוא דרך לציורי הקיר המפורטים בספר אם תצעד אחרי הצקבות הצהובים המסומנים צל המדרכות.

ביקור נצים

The CHEMAINUS MURALS

Festival of Murals

Published by
THE CHEMAINUS FESTIVAL OF MURALS
SOCIETY, P.O. BOX 1311, 9796 WILLOW ST.,
CHEMAINUS, B.C. CANADA V0R 1K0

ISBN # 0-9693161-2-7

1998 EDITORIAL CO-ORDINATOR
C. GREIG-MANNING

EDITORIAL TEAM
1998 – GEORGE BAILEY, IRENE DUTTON,
IRENE HUDAK, FRANK KERR,
WILLIAM MANNING, LINDA TUCKER

1993 – VIRGINA BLATCHFORD,
MARIE BURROUGHS, IRENE DUTTON,
BONNEY KING, BARBARA SAPERGIA,
KARL SCHUTZ

ART DIRECTION & DESIGN
IMAGECRAFT STUDIO LIMITED

WRITERS
CYNTHIA BUNBURY
GREGG PERRY

PHOTO CREDITS
LORNE GREEN, LES POLOSKEY,
D. CLINE, PAUL FLETCHER, FUZZY HARRISON,
KIFF HOLLAND, PROF. J.E.L. ROBERTSON,
BRANDON WALKER, TOM WALKER, PAUL WALTERS
AND MANY OTHER CHEMAINIACS

PRODUCTION
IMAGECRAFT, LANDSEND, SGM

FILM HOUSE SERVICES & PRINTING
FLEMING PRINTING LIMITED

TO ORDER THIS BOOK FROM
THE FESTIVAL OF MURALS SOCIETY
PHONE: (250) 246-4701 • FAX: (250) 246-3251
WRITE: P.O. BOX 1311
CHEMAINUS, B.C.
CANADA V0R IK0
OR EMAIL abc@tourism.chemainus.bc.ca

CONTENTS

*C*hemainus is appropriately known as "The Little Town That Did"©. The thriving, bustling community that it is today is a credit to the community, many enthusiastic local business people, and hundreds of volunteers, who rose to the challenge to create a new economic base for their community when the town's mill laid off hundreds of workers. The hard work, dedication and determination of these people made Chemainus well known throughout Canada and the international community as the 'Town of Murals'.

I am proud to represent this community as its member of the provincial legislature and I am pleased to extend a warm welcome to visitors from all around the world who will come and share our celebrations.

Welcome to "The Little Town That Did"©.

Yours sincerely,

Jan Pullinger, MLA
Cowichan-Ladysmith

*O*ur giant outdoor art gallery has captured the hearts of people from all over the world. The famous Chemainus murals have indeed proven what determination, energy, and enthusiasm can accomplish. From a little town solely dependent on the forest industry, Chemainus is now a multi-faceted community bursting with charm and atmosphere.

On behalf of the District of North Cowichan Council, I invite you to experience the magic of Chemainus. You will not forget the enchanting paintings that tell of our humble beginnings, the excellent service of our many specialty shops, or the warmth and hospitality of our residents. Come and visit our corner of the world – you'll be glad you did!

Anne Murray
Mayor

CHEMAINUS

The Little Town That Did!©

From just five murals and lots of spirit in the summer of 1982, Chemainus has struggled, grown and succeeded in literally putting itself on the map. In 1983, it won the prestigious New York Downtown Revitalization Award for its redevelopment of the town core. It has since gained world-wide acclaim for the integrity and superb artistry of its huge depictions of the town's history.

Thirty-three larger-than-life historic paintings in this open air gallery now greet the gaze of thousands of visitors each year. Chemainus thrives as a result, but it remains a small town, with just over 3,500 residents. These welcoming people still dish out island hospitality, along with ice cream and afternoon tea and scones just as they always have. Chemainus really is "the little town that did"©.

The coastal community of Chemainus has a rich and varied history. Beginning thousands of years ago with the Coast Salish Native people, that history has flourished through a century and a half of industry and labour. With a mild climate and a great abundance of natural resources, the surrounding area became home to many hardworking settlers. Side by side, these people hewed a town of some substance from the majestic forests.

These same forests have provided the lifeblood of the entire valley for more than a century now, but to Chemainus, this has

PAUL FLETCHER / VISIONQUEST

tired-looking main street. Planters overflowing with fresh flowers, new benches, improved public spaces and better parking facilities, all resulted from this initial project. Suddenly though, the town faced much graver problems than a lack of fresh paint along its thoroughfares. After more than 120 years the mill shut down in 1983.

Without waiting to hear if the mill would reopen, residents rallied to hold on to the roots they had established here. They continued the beautification of the central core. But more was to come. With the remarkable energy and creative vision of resident and businessman Karl Schutz, and the committed support of the then-mayor Graham Bruce and the municipal council, the Festival of Murals Association was born. The painting of murals on some of the outside walls of local buildings was

the Municipality of North Cowichan's colourful investment in a livelier looking village.

Those early years of redevelopment now seem a part of history, too. More than a quarter of a million dollars has been invested in the mural project by private, corporate, federal, provincial and municipal investors. As a direct result, Chemainus has attracted in excess of one hundred new businesses, 350-450,000 visitors a year and a $3.5 million dinner theatre. From a dependence on a single industry, it has broadened its economic base to offer a range of service and tourist related activities. To everyone's relief, the mill was rebuilt and modernized, and reopened in 1985. By that time, residents and visitors alike felt that they had proven they could survive the worst of times through their spirit and determination.

The town now has a new look. It is one that is reminis-cent of past glories, and the result is a pleasing mixture of Victorian and frontier design, with a real

down home feel. Chemainus welcomes you to a feast for all the senses. Come and taste the magic! You'll never experience history quite like this again.

"Obviously, Chemainus, B.C., no matter how small it is, has things like imagination and foresight and a willingness on the part of its residents and community leaders to get behind daring and adventurous initiatives."

-- Author and historian, Pierre Berton.

---

sometimes been a painful reality.

In 1981 the town of Chemainus benefited from a province wide redevelop-ment fund, and initiated a downtown revitalization project to give a face lift to a

Chemainus chief Clay-sa-luke (far left)

Chemainus townsite on the ocean with Chemainus Valley in background (middle)

Chemainus Theatre – offering exciting live theatre, dining, and an art gallery all under one roof! (left)

Sawmill worker with logs in boom awaiting processing (right)

The Inspiration Of It All!

Water Over The Wheel - The story of the Chemainus Valley and its people.
by W.H. Olsen.

It is fortunate indeed that the Chemainus area was blessed with a chronicler of strong determination. The late W.H. (Harry) Olsen brought a rare combination of talent and ability to the task of writing Water Over The Wheel, the book on which the theme of the Chemainus Festival of Murals is based.

Aided by his wife, Catherine, Olsen pieced together tales and fact, pored over archives and records, sorted myth from reality, to create a time-capsule of the Chemainus Valley.

Unlike many historians who begin their stories with the arrival of the white settlers to an area, Mr. Olsen devotes much of his book to the fascinating and important Native history of the area. Here are the ingredients of a fascinating yarn - the danger and mystery of a wilderness land, the dignity, struggle and sometimes savagery of Native life, the toil and heartbreak of early European pioneers, a generous sprinkling of humour and a unique, century old partnership between a community and an industry. In the words of Willard E. Ireland, Provincial Librarian and Archivist, *"It is a story well worth the telling! It is a privilege to recommend Water Over the Wheel to you."*

Olsen's warm and factual book has been an encouragement and a source of inspiration for the people of Chemainus.

The Book that started it all, Water over the Wheel – The story of The Chemainus Valley and its people by W.H. Olsen. (below). Steam Donkey and crew cutting Chemainus Valley fir circa 1900 (right).

They have rediscovered the power of their own roots, and have translated it into a living example of how that past is a unique part of their present, indeed their future.

The Story of Chemainus
Produced by Casson Studios
in conjunction with

the Arts and Business Council of Chemainus
"If you believe it, you can achieve great things." The encouraging history of one of North America's most successful community rejuvenations underscores this theme in this heart-warming video.

Recounted by a gentle grandfather to his aspiring ballerina granddaughter

group or individual with a dream worth achieving.

The Spirit Of Chemainus Lives On....

One of the many offshoots of the Chemainus Festival of Murals project was

pality of North Cowichan, as well as other donors.

Launched in Chemainus on September 14, 1985, and rigged in Victoria harbour, her 225 square meters (2500 sq. ft.) of sails were made on Galiano Island, and her blocks and dead-eyes came from Lunenberg, Nova Scotia. Everything about her is handcrafted. Even the portholes had to be custom cast. There are berths for 20 sail trainees and four crew.

The film crew on sight, shooting (left). Artisan at work honing timber for Spirit Of Chemainus (right). Rigged and flying her colours in Victoria Inner Harbour (below).

as she faces the challenge of a dance recital, *The Story of Chemainus* honours the determination of this little town to begin again creatively in the face of adverse economic conditions.

The partnership of the people, the artists, the business community and the government is presented as a model of hope for other small towns, and, indeed, for any

the building of the brigantine Spirit of Chemainus in 1984-85.

The vessel is designed after the Hudson Bay Company's Cadboro, the first vessel to sail into Victoria Harbour in 1837. The Spirit of Chemainus is named in honour of the Vancouver Island town where she was built by and for the Sail and Life Training Society of Victoria, with the support of then-Mayor Graham Bruce and council, the citizens and businesses of the Munici-

The Vision and The Visionaries

*"When your back is to the wall,
Why not simply turn around
And paint it all..."*

ALLEN DESNOYERS, *Over Deepest Blue*

After being a one-resource town for over a century, Chemainus was up against the wall of a changing world, where new technologies and economic shifts threatened to leave this little town behind and disrupt the security of families who had depended all their lives on the forest industry.

The newly elected young mayor of North Cowichan, Graham Bruce, was keen to encourage diversity and new directions that would keep the communities in the Chemainus and Cowichan Valleys productive and stable places to live. He knew it would depend upon the initiative of the people themselves to do something of their own volition without waiting for the government. Already, many Chemainus residents had been discussing the issues, without result.

As the decade of the eighties dawned, Mayor Bruce invited interested business people to consider taking advantage of the provincial government's Downtown Revitalization Programme. Chemainus was the first BC community to respond, and the Chemainus Revitalization Committee was formed:

- Al Johnson, (chairman) grocer;
- Vern Kay, hardware retailer;
- Joe Hudak, druggist;
- Bill Jameson, furniture retailer;
- Jack Jameson, furniture retailer;
- Joe Jeles, appliance retailer;
- Tony Monco, restaurateur.

This "Group of Seven", as it was dubbed, formed the core of an active group of volunteers, men and women, who envisioned a new face and expanded economic opportunities for Chemainus. They chose tourism as the best adjunct to logging in the future that they pictured for their little town. It seemed a natural choice to promote the logging theme, and they asked Carl Wrigley, a retired senior, to produce some conceptual drawings of how the Chemainus story could be portrayed in murals, thus establishing their future direction.

The municipality then made an inspired decision to hire a long time Chemainus resident, Karl Schutz, as the coordinator of the revitalization project. Schutz undertook the feasibility study for a new look for the downtown core. He too was convinced that celebrating the history and heritage of Chemainus would work wonders on the spirit of the community and attract attention from all over the world. Wisely, he insisted that recognized artists paint the murals, thereby creating a distinguished outdoor gallery.

Schutz and the Group of Seven launched the programme that accomplished the transformation of the downtown buildings into an attractive market for visitors, as well as for artisans and other merchants. The painting of the first murals in 1982 attracted new crowds, and the artists themselves were a major part of the fascination.

Wanting a separate body to over-see and preserve the enduring legacy of the murals, Schutz pushed for the creation of the Festival of Murals Society, and became its first Executive Director. Catherine Fyffe, a third generation Chemainus resident, became the first Festival administrator.

Karl's irrepressible energy earned for him inclusion among the Fifty Canadian Men of Influence for 1987. By 1988, the Province recognized his contribution, not just to Chemainus, but also to Vancouver Island and British Columbia, appointing him an Ambassador of Tourism for the Province. In 1992, Her Majesty the Queen authorized a Commemorative Medal to mark the 125th anniversary of Confederation, honouring Canadians who have made a special contribution to their community and their country. Karl Schutz was one of those Canadians so honoured.

For over ten years now, the Festival of Murals has been operated principally by dedicated volunteers, producing the last 23 murals. These unnamed individuals have been honoured by visitors from around the globe who consistently express delight in their experience.

These honours are shared by all the men and women of Chemainus who have participated in making this vision a reality. The Spirit of Chemainus stands as a portrait of hope for all small communities in the next millennium.

MURALS

Steam Donkey At Work

Painted in 1982 by Frank Lewis and Nancy Lagana, Victoria, B.C.

8.1M X 3M (27' X 10'), WILLOW STREET

The Artists

Originally from Victoria, B.C., Frank Lewis' career took him eastward in the late 1950's. Soon he was winning acclaim for his work as a professional illustrator, with awards from both Toronto and Montreal. In 1963, his work was placed in the prestigious New York Society of Illustrators Show.

Back on the West Coast in the late 1960s, the style of Lewis' painting began to change and evolve on a larger scale, beginning with the decoration of a construction fence at the Vancouver Court House. Soon to come were mural paintings for tourism projects, as well as commissioned works for Daon Corporation, the Carnegie Library, the Westerly Hotel, and other clients.

As Lewis' assistant, Nancy Lagana brought with her an impressive academic art background. She has an Honours B.A. from Harvard University, and studied ceramics and sculpture at the Vancouver School of Art.

The Art

For the steam donkey and its crew, hauling a log from the forest was an obstacle course of the worst kind, fighting rocks, gullies, and stumps every inch of the way.

"Charlie", the line horse waited patiently in the background, ready to pull the 20mm cable to the next felled log.

The steam donkey was invented by John Dolbeer in 1882. This particular one was built by Murray Bros. in San Francisco and started work for the Victoria Lumber & Manufacturing Company in Chemainus in 1885. The painting is based on a photograph from 1902. The man controlling the lever on the steam donkey is

Herbert M. Olsen, who was later to become prominent in world-wide lumbering ventures.

Now restored, this Dolbeer steam donkey has been retired to the B.C. Forest Museum in the Cowichan Valley.

Sketch Proposal by Frank Lewis (left)

The Thirty-Three Metre Collage

33M X 4.2 M (108' X 14'), LEGION STREET

Painted in 1982 by Frank Lewis and Nancy Lagana (left and centre) and Paul Marcano (right)

The Art

On the left, a crew of stevedores at the Chemainus wharf stands before a fully rigged ship, her sails clewed up for drying. Based on a photograph from 1901, the scene is typical of the busy harbour on any given day. Sailing ships and steamers, as

many as five at a time, would be loading or waiting to begin their "lay days".

At the centre, a boomman sorts logs in the slippery danger of the log dump. The mill is portrayed here as it was in 1892; it was the third operation to be built on the site. Owned by the Victoria Lumber and Manufacturing Company Limited, it was improved over the years until a fire destroyed it in 1923.

On the right, Engine No. 21 of the V.L. & M. Company rolls off another load into the Chemainus log dump. The year is 1899. The locomotive, a 2-8-0, has already seen two decades of work having been built for the Pennsylvania Railroad as Engine No. 248 in 1879 (CN 433).

Steam Train On Bridge Over Chemainus River

Painted in 1982 by Paul Marcano, Victoria, B.C.

16.3M X 6.6M (53' X 22'), CYPRUS STREET

The Artist

From the hills of eastern Ontario, Paul Marcano's artist parents influenced their gifted son to create from his inner vision. Since then, Marcano has developed into an interpreter of life, and his repertoire ranges from surrealistic landscapes to fluorescent images and self-portraits. He is also a musician, having recorded an album entitled "Islands in Space", which he calls the "auditory version of my vision".

Marcano's first project for Chemainus was to paint one-third of the grand Thirty-three Metre Collage. The final product there convinced Festival of Murals organizers to commission him to do a second, and then a third mural. The precision of his trompe l'oeil effect of the Hong Hing Corner Store, and Locomotive No. 4 crossing the bridge are fine examples of his meticulous style and skilled use of the airbrush.

The Art

Thundering across a log bridge over the Chemainus River is Locomotive No.4, an 80-ton Porter 2-6-2T, once the pride of the Victoria Lumber & Manufacturing Company's Copper Canyon Railway System. Chemainus was the delivery point of the first, the last, and the longest enduring rail logging operation in British Columbia.

"Copper Canyon Railway"

The Hong Hing Waterfront Store

Painted in 1982 by Paul Marcano, Victoria, B.C.

8M X 4.4M (26' X 15'), CORNER OF OAK AND ESPLANADE STREETS

The Art

Fong Yen Lew was known to almost everyone as Hong Hing, the name he gave to his store. Born in the late 1800s, he came to Canada, and set up his business in Chemainus around 1915. His enterprise began as a laundry, but he later sold groceries, chickens and second-hand goods. Eventually, he expanded into bootlegging and running a gambling house.

Hong Hing was welcome everywhere in Chemainus, just as he welcomed everyone. His easy credit terms and kind heart probably lost him plenty of money over the years, but it gained him many friends.

Hong Hing's "Truck" (left) and his "Story" (right) was added in 1983 by Dan Sawatzky

Historic photo by Stuart Clement (right).

In the 1950's, the opening of a government liquor store in Chemainus foretold the demise of Hong Hing's establishment. His original building was eventually declared a fire trap and demolished. Hong Hing returned to China, presumably to die. But to the surprise of only a few who did not know him, he instead married a woman 40 years his junior, who eventually presented him with an heir.

Fallers Undercutting A Fir

Painted in 1982 by Thomas Robertson, Edinburgh, Scotland

3.8M X 10M (12' X 33'), FIREHALL TOWER, CYPRUS STREET

The Artist

Trained as a fine art restorer, conservator and guilder by the long-established firm of Aitken, Dott and Son in Edinburgh, Thomas Robertson was encouraged through his experience to become an artist himself.

Leaving his native Scotland, he studied at the Epsom School of Art and Design in England, gaining expertise in screen printing as well as developing his hand as a portrait artist and landscape painter. While visiting Vancouver Island in 1982,

Robertson found himself drawn in by the mural project. He volunteered his time, energy and artistic skill in executing the fourth mural in the endeavour, to be painted on the Fire Hall Tower.

Fallers Undercutting a Fir was Robertson's first larger-than-life painting.

The Art

Working as a team, fallers cutting a coastal giant had to stand at the same elevation. This was made almost impossible by the rough ground and steep slopes of the rainforest. To overcome the difference in heights, and to get above the sometimes massive flaring butt of a tree, springboards were used.

Made from yellow cedar planks, and iron tipped, these were wedged into notches in the tree. Each faller would stand upon a springboard, and wield his double-edged falling axe with precision. A thin-bladed two handled cross-cut saw, eight feet in length, was shared between them to complete the job.

Dangling from the lower part of the tree being cut was an oil bottle with a sharp hook fastened to its neck. It was often corked with a piece of grooved fir bark. When the saw complained with the heat of friction, oil would be sprinkled along the blade.

Arrival Of The 'Reindeer' In Horseshoe Bay

Painted in 1983 by Sandy Clark and Lea Goward, Victoria, B.C.

7.7M X 4.6M (25' X 13'), MILL STREET

The Artists

Though born and raised in Ontario, Sandy Clark's artistic inspiration is largely drawn from the particular moods and atmosphere of the sea. More than fifteen years ago Clark came west from Toronto, bringing with her a superb understanding of the intricacies of water-borne vessels, as well as an innate ability to interpret people and their distinct expressions.

Clark paints in oil and watercolour to create impressions of individuals she has met and of moments of peace experienced on ocean shores. She has exhibited in British Columbia, the United States and Australia.

While attending the University of Victoria, Lea Goward experienced large-scale painting first hand in a "theatre-in-education" program. She put her new knowledge to work as Sandy Clark's assistant for the painting of Arrival of the 'Reindeer' in Horseshoe Bay. Goward, a native of Kamloops, B.C., now works in pastels, watercolour, and conte.

Lea Goward (left) and Sandy Clark.

The Art

A luminescent cedar bark cloak envelops the figure of a Native princess as she contemplates the arrival of the sloop Her Majesty's Ship Reindeer. The ship's commander, Captain A. E. Kennedy, was an acquaintance of Isabel and Thomas George Askew, pioneers of Chemainus and mill owners for many years. The Reindeer made regular stops in Horseshoe Bay (now called Chemainus Bay) on its rounds of the coast.

Logging With Oxen

Painted in 1983 by Harold Lyon, Fountain Hills, Arizona

8.4 M X 3.7M (60' X 12'), WATER WHEEL PARKING LOT

The Artist

Harold Lyon grew up in Ontario, surrounded by cattle and horses. He worked in the bush, sawing logs, and so developed a solid background on which to base his strong portrayals of rugged bush life. As an artist, Lyon has a special penchant for things "Western" - the round-ups, cowboys and weather-worn faces in windswept settings.

Lyon attended art college in Detroit and Toronto, then worked as a graphic artist and set designer. For a time he was the Art Director for the Hudson Bay Company in Calgary. He worked for five years as an illustrator in Seattle before returning to Canada to live and paint in the Okanagan. Harold is presently living in Fountain Hills, Arizona.

Logging with Oxen is a wonderful example of Lyon's inherent energy, imbued as it is with a sense of the slow plodding and strain of the powerful animals harnessed to massive logs.

Harold Lyon's paintings are exhibited in galleries in Canada and the United States. He painted the portrait of the former Lieutenant-Governor of British Columbia, and his latest series of Arctic scenes has toured the country.

The Art

Around 1898, oxen were the main form of power in logging, where good timber was available. "Large, well-equipped outfits used twenty to twenty-four oxen. These were divided into two teams: one drawing the logs from the bush to the road, while the other and stronger team was employed in skidding the logs to the water. Crude roads were made and small logs embedded skillfully athwart them at

8-foot intervals. These were the skid-roads over which the oxen draw the logs to the sea." (R.I. Dougan, from Cowichan My Valley)

Since the ox's hoof has a thin shell, the oxen were carefully shod with thin, half-moon shaped iron shoes. The job of shoeing the oxen was done on Sundays or after hours by the "teamsters", with assistance from a young helper, the "greaser".

Chemainus 1891

Painted in 1983 by David Maclagan

16.4M X 3.5M (54' X 12'), MILL STREET

The Artist

With over 40 murals to his credit, David Maclagan is no stranger to mural art. One of his larger undertakings is an historical tableau which measures 120 feet in length, at the Yukon Territorial Legislative Buildings in Whitehorse.

Maclagan is from Ontario, where he graduated from the Ontario College of Art. He has been a professional artist, designer and instructor since 1957, and is currently a teacher at Capilano College in North Vancouver.

The gentle, warm tones of Maclagan's panorama are rendered more powerful by the bold strokes of his broad brush. He has created a composite painting based on a number of sepia tone photographs from 1891, showing both the labour and the leisure of early residents.

David Maclagan's paintings hang in many collections in Canada, the United States and Japan.

The Art

The mural shows the original town of Chemainus, then known as Horseshoe Bay. Passenger cars of the famous Esquimalt and Nanaimo Railway (E&N) steam their way across this scene of the settlement at Horseshoe Bay in 1891.

The large white house on the far left was the mill manager's residence. The area is now Waterwheel Park. The predominant centre road is present-day Mill Street, with Saint Michael and All Angels Anglican Church, erected in 1891 by Rev. David Holmes, situated on the mid-right.

Across from the railway station, on the right side of Mill Street in the foreground, was the Conway House and telegraph office. Heritage Square now occupies that site.

9

Camp 2 On A Sunday

Painted in 1983 by David J. More, Red Deer, Alberta

6.5M X 6.3M (21' X 20'), WATER WHEEL CRESCENT

The Artist

As a graduate in Fine Arts (Painting) from the Alberta College of Art in 1972, David More's background did not include murals. But his methodical approach and tenacity helped him tackle Camp 2 On a Sunday and produced layers of rich hues indicative of the ambience of a forest morning.

Born in Scotland, More grew up in Alberta and pursued his artistic career in that province. He has worked for Alberta Culture and independently, as well as instructing drawing, painting and design at the Alberta College of Art. He has also co-authored and illustrated four books with Vancouver author and humourist Eric Nicol.

More's oil, acrylic and mixed media paintings and drawings are found in the Alberta Art Foundation, the Canada Council Art Bank and numerous private and corporate collections.

The Art

Loggers at the V.L. & M. Company's Camp 2 (circa 1902) would spend part of their Sundays around the bunkhouse. It was the day for washing up, and tending to one's personal grooming. Half barrels and four-gallon coal-oil cans were used as washtubs, while a rail spike keg made a great barber's chair.

At about this time, mining fever erupted, with rich strikes of gold and copper resulting in new mining operations opening up at Mount Sicker, Tyee and Lenora. These competed for the loggers' labour and commitment to the company.

Company Store

Painted in 1983 by Dan Sawatzky, Chemainus, B.C.

10M X 8M (30' X 16'), WATER WHEEL CRESCENT

The Artist

"There's no place in the world I'd rather be! I can feel the sparkle in the air just approaching the town. I've never been so involved in a community."

Born in Vancouver and raised in Castlegar, B.C., Dan Sawatzky has experienced much of what British Columbia has to offer. His travels have accorded him a sense of locale which he has translated into art. His main objective is accurately depicting the humble qualities of everyday objects that are so much a part of our heritage.

Largely self taught, Sawatzky's repertoire includes works in pen and ink and egg tempera. On a larger scale he has painted historical murals all across North America, both in Canada and the U.S.A.

He and his growing family have made their home in Chemainus since he painted the mural Company Store. These days Dan works from his studio in his Victorian styled home and remains active in ongoing community endeavours.

The Art

Using an oval format, this mural shows an interior depiction of the Victoria Lumber & Manufacturing Company Store, circa 1917. The artist recreated the deep perspective of the colourfully-laden shelves from old photographs.

D.A. Gatus was the manager. He is seen standing in the mid-ground. Miss Ann Porter worked as a clerk, and is pictured on the left behind the counter.

Artist's proposal (below)

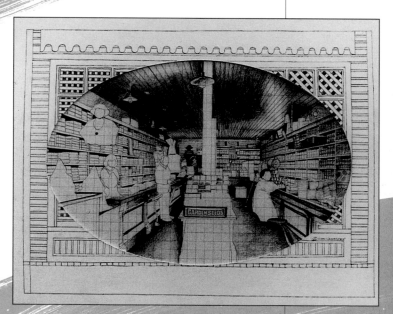

The V.L. & M. Company used one of the first known credit card systems in the store. The purchaser would pay for the goods with coupons. In turn, the store would receive credit for the same from the company, which would deduct the amount from their employee's pay cheque.

The name "Victoria Lumber & Manufacturing Company", and its trade mark, the letter "V" in a diamond, became known throughout the world.

Temporary Homes

Painted in 1983 by David White, Nassau, Bahamas

5.8M X 4M (19' X 13'), MILL STREET & CHEMAINUS ROAD

The Artist

Hailing from Hove, Sussex, England, and a graduate of the architecture program at Brighton College of Arts and Crafts, David White began his creative career designing buildings in England, New York and the Bahamas.

He has since developed into an artist of some renown, has instructed art and is past president of the Federation of Canadian Artists. White's skill as a watercolourist is clearly evident in his fine depiction of the harsh realities of life in a stark wilderness.

As well as having won several awards, White's paintings adorn many private and corporate collections in Canada, the United States and the Bahamas.

The Art

Such rudimentary accomodation was not new to communities like Chemainus. Many early settlers to the area lived in similar wall tents for their initial stay, as

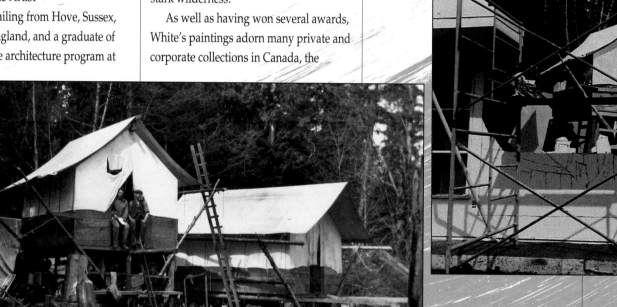

ROAD CONSTRUCTION CAMP
1912

they struggled to clear land and gather precious funds and materials to build better lodgings.

In the early years of this century, the mining boom had caused a rapid rise in population throughout the Chemainus area. Workers could be seen constructing these rough structures built from local timber and canvas.

Road construction camps such as the one pictured here were a common sight, as new roads were pushed through rugged wilderness. This particular camp was located north of Chemainus, near Saltair (formerly Wilson's Crossing) in 1912.

Wall tents continue to be used in remote locations in British Columbia to house staff on small mining exploration projects. They remain a quick, simple and effective method of accomodating workers for a short time in difficult conditions.

Native Heritage

Painted in 1983 by Paul Ygartua, Vancouver, B.C.

15.4M X 6.2M (50' X 20'), MILL STREET & CHEMAINUS ROAD

The Artist

"Over the years, it really seems that a guiding hand is directing me to create a tableau, portraying nomadic people-with their differences and similarities".

Faces have haunted Paul Ygartua throughout his artistic life. They have also brought him international recognition. His travels to Europe, South America and Western Canada have led him to paint the strength, dignity and struggle of native and ethnic peoples of the world.

Ygartua is of Basque heritage, but was born in northern England. He earned a degree in Industrial Design from Liverpool College, and is a member of the Guild of Gold and Silversmithing. His beginnings as a jewellery designer soon gave way to the more powerful images of the first peoples he is now known for.

He won universal acclaim for his Native Heritage series, and his paintings have been exhibited in Western Europe, the Middle East, the United States and Japan. One of his finest works graced the exterior walls of the United Nations Pavilion at the world exposition (Expo '86) in Vancouver.

The Art

This immense mural is based on figures from the Native past and present in this area. Carved poles flank the central images of (left) Ce-who-latza, who was chief of the Lyakun Village on Shingle Point, Valdez Island, as well as a constable of the Native Police and a Native pilot for the Royal Navy; (centre) former Chemainus Band Chief Clay-sa-luke; and (right) a Salish woman. Among the other figures who appear is Mrs. Mary Rice, top right.

A dozen bands of Cowichan people, part of the Coast Salish language group, occupied the Cowichan and Chemainus valleys for many hundreds of years before Europeans came to settle the area. Here they developed the rich heritage and superb artistic traditions which they maintain today. Many descendants of these first people continue to live in and around Chemainus.

Billy Thomas

Painted in 1984 by Sandy Clark, Victoria, B.C.

2.1M X 2.4M (7' X 8'), WILLOW STREET

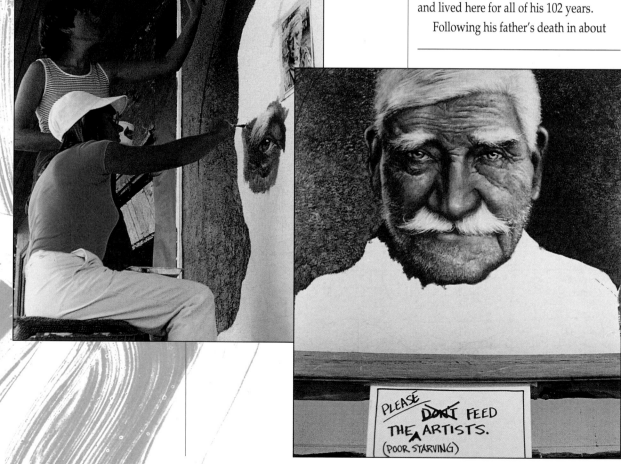

The Artist

Once again applying her skill and insight, Victoria artist Sandy Clark brings alive one of Chemainus' most loved characters.

The Art

William Ishmael (Billy) Thomas was born to William and Catherine Thomas in 1874. He was the first male child of European ancestry born in the Chemainus Valley, and lived here for all of his 102 years.

Following his father's death in about 1878, his mother remarried, to William Alexander Miller. The log cabin fronting the Chemainus River which had served as their home was eventually replaced by a larger farmhouse. It was the house Billy would live in all his life.

Although he surveyed for a time, Billy mostly earned his living from his 300 acres of land. He sold wood, some to help build the Chemainus River bridge, on which he worked. Some of it went to the sawmill, and some went to private customers. He and his sister raised cows, and sold milk and cream locally. Billy also raised heavy horses - Clydesdales. At the point where he could have made a little money from the sale of the beasts, trains and trucks took over the transportation business.

Billy could recall many things in his later years. He remembered the building of the railway, the rerouting of the first highway because the oxen got stuck in mud near the river. He had vivid memories of all the payrolls that had ever been stolen from a train or coach. He recalled the long day's ride to Nanaimo for supplies, and he even remembered the days when supplies came by boat.

Billy Thomas is fondly remembered by many Valley residents, and they think he would have been very pleased to know his picture is part of the mural project of Chemainus.

14

H.M.S. Forward

Painted in 1984 by Harry Heine R.S.M.A., F.C.A., C.S.M.A.

9.8M X 2.6M (32' X 8.5'), MILL STREET

The Artist
Born in Edmonton, Alberta, Harry Heine became a successful commercial artist and illustrator. In 1970 he moved to British Columbia's Vancouver Island and launched a career as a marine artist. He was elected to the Federation of Canadian Artists (FCA) as a senior member in 1979, and in 1980 he became the first Canadian to be elected to the Royal Society of Marine Artists (RSMA), a group of less than 50 international painters based in London, England.

His paintings hang in permanent collections such as Mystic Seaport Museum, Connecticut; the Mendel Gallery, Saskatchewan; the Captain Cook Birthplace Museum, England; the Provincial Maritime Museum, British Columbia; the Washington State Arts Commission; the Government House Collection, British Columbia; the Shell Canada Collection; and the National Maritime Museum, England.

Heine is a Charter Member of the Canadian Society of Marine Artists (CSMA) and is a past vice-president of that

Society and of the FCA. In 1983 he was named as an Honorary Alberta Artist, and in 1985 he became an Honorary Citizen of the City of Victoria and an Honorary Crew Member of Canada 1, Canada's entry in the America's Cup yacht race.

The Art
The gunboat H.M.S. Forward was one of four such Royal Navy vessels dispatched during the search for the murderers of William Brady and the Marks family in April, 1863. The murder had taken place on Saturna Island to the south, but the fugitives were eventually apprehended only after a search and siege operation of more than two weeks, which included Thetis and Kuper Islands just off Chemainus harbour.

Chemainus Tug Boat

Painted in 1984 by Mark Heine and Harry Heine

30.5M X 13M (10.5' X 43'), LEGION STREET

The Artists

Mark Heine spent his early childhood in Alberta, and then moved with his family to Vancouver Island in 1970. During his school years, he achieved some success with his art work, winning several poster contests. These included the Canadian Cancer Society competition, which he captured twice, and a scholarship award from the Department of the Attorney-General for his "Counterattack" entry.

The younger Heine attended Capilano College in North Vancouver, and then travelled for a time in Europe before setting his hand to mural painting. He has been part of mural painting in Fort Saskatchewan, Vegreville, and Fort McMurray, Alberta. In 1986, he was responsible for two murals for the U.S. Pavilion at Expo 86 in Vancouver. At present, Mark Heine is a graphic artist in Vancouver, is a member of the Renaissance Artist Society, and sits on the board of the Canadian Association of Artists and Illustrators.

The Art

The tug boat Chemainus was built at Chemainus in 1909 for the Victoria Lumber & Manufacturing Company Limited. Equipped with a coal burning engine (this was changed to oil in the 1920s) she was 26.8 metres (93 feet) long with a 6.4 metre (22-foot) beam, and a depth of 2.9 metres (10 feet). On November 14, 1911, she caught fire at the coal bunkers in Coal Harbour, Vancouver, and burned to the water's edge. She was salvaged in December and rebuilt. After being sold in 1918 to Kingcome Navigation Co. Ltd., she was brought back to Chemainus in 1923 by the Chemainus Towing Co. Ltd.. Then on November 24, 1945, she ran aground at Copelan Island (Ragged Island), and was written off as a total loss.

The first recorded export of lumber from Chemainus was on September 25, 1863.

Hard labour was the order of the day as the Chinese "Bull Gang" moved the big timber on a two wheeled cart from the yard to the sailing vessel. Planks laid in front of the wheels provided a smooth track.

1884 Chinese Bull Gang

Painted in 1984 by Ernest Marza, Victoria, B.C.

32M X 3M (104' X 10'), LEGION STREET

The Artist

"I am from Transylvania, that part of Romania that inspired the mural project here in Chemainus. You might say that my connection with the murals is a very strong one!"

Before emigrating to Canada in 1956, Ernest Marza has spent most of his working life as a painter and sculptor in eastern Europe. He pursued his chosen career once here, supplementing it with studies at the Kootenay School of Art in B.C. He then specialized in the art of restoration and conservation at San Miguel

de Allende in Mexico and at Sanomo, California.

Marza now works as an artist, teacher, and restorer in Victoria, where he has had a long association with the "Little Gallery". His paintings can be found in private collections throughout Canada, the U.S. and Germany, as well as in the permanent collections of Gulf Oil, B.C. Hydro and other corporations.

The Art
Many Chinese people had been enticed to the west coast of Canada as labourers in the late 1800s. A number settled in Chemainus with the promise of steady work in the lumber industry. In the painting, twenty-three men of the Chinese "Bull Gang" struggle to move a huge timber through the lumber yard to a sailing vessel. Planks laid in front of the wheels of the cart provided a smooth track. The mural is based on a photograph from the Victoria Lumber & Manufacturing Company at the turn of the century.

First Schoolhouse, 1883

Painted in 1986 by Kiff Holland F.C.A., C.S.M.A., R.I, (HON.)

4.825M X 2.44M (15'10" X 8'), WEST WALL, WILLOW STREET PLACE

The Artist

Born in South Africa, Kiff Holland received his formal art training at the University of Witwatersrand and at the Johannesburg School of Art. He chose to immigrate to Canada in 1975 and soon discovered the new spectrum of soft colours and ethereal hues offered by this northern land.

The artist's ardour for juxtaposing luminous colours can be found in his mural, First School House, 1883. The calculated interaction of texture, light and the flickering network of colour patches demonstrates the influence that both Bahaus and the impressionists had on Holland's artistic development.

Kiff Holland's works in acrylic, watercolour and oil have been exhibited at the British Institute of Painters in Watercolour and the Royal Society of British Artists. His paintings can be found in galleries in North America and South Africa.

The Art

In 1883, the first public school in Chemainus was built next to the route of the E. & N. Railway. The mural is based on an 1885 photograph.

In the background is Samuel Girdlestone Lewis, the first local school teacher. He also ran a number of local businesses. From left to right in the foreground are Jack Windsor, Fred Cottenham, Elsie and Charlie Campbell, Mary Windsor, William Thomas, George, Lillie, Fred and Tom Bonsall and Joe Allard.

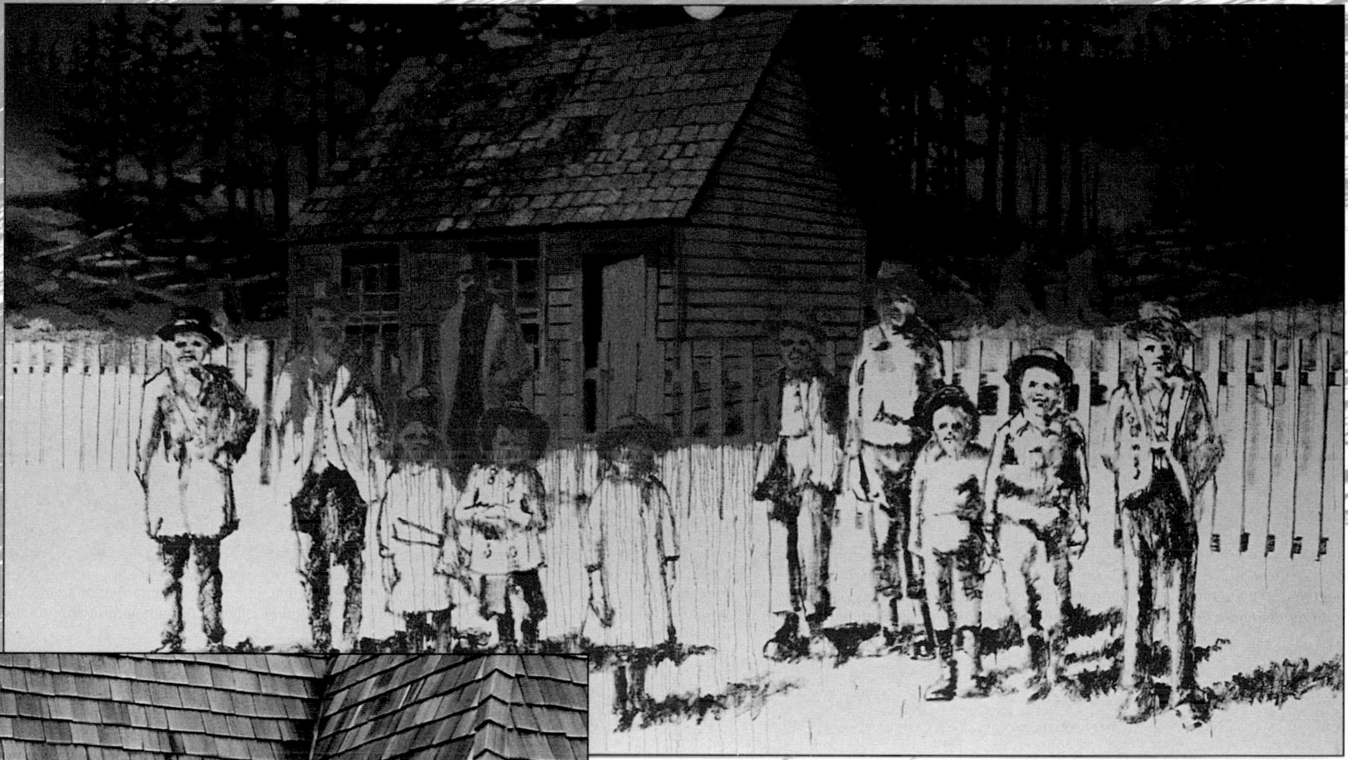

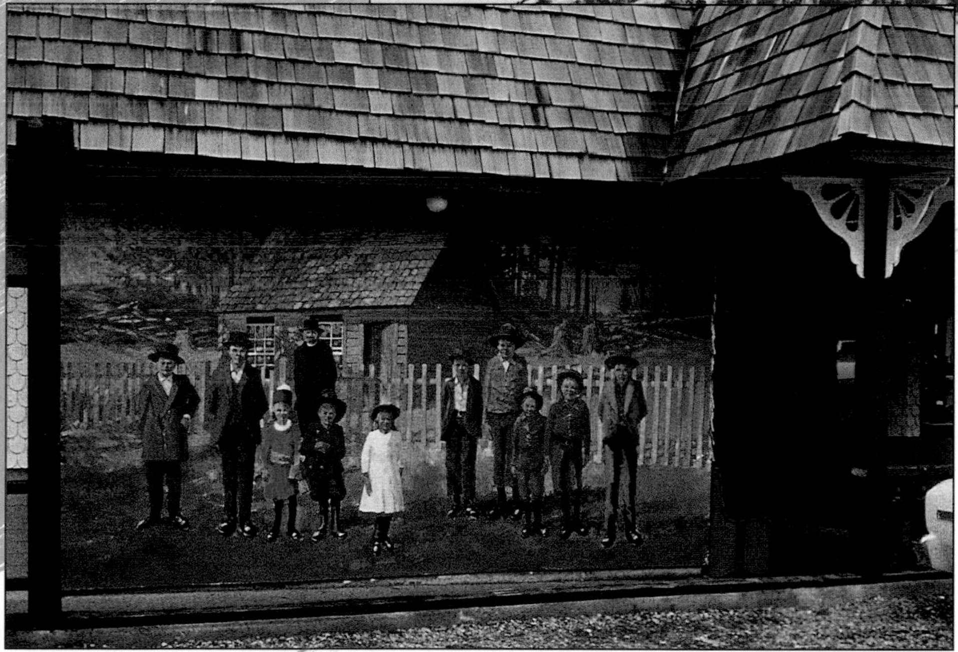

Julia Askew - First Child Of European Ancestry Born In The Chemainus Valley

Painted in 1986 by Elizabeth Smily, West Vancouver, B.C.

3.05M X 1.5M (10' X 5'), MILL STREET

The Artist

Upon graduating from the Royal Academy School in London in 1949, Elizabeth Smily won the Lord Leverhulme award, accorded the best student in painting, sculpture or architecture. Three years later, she moved to Montreal, where she taught portraiture and life drawing. During her stay, she exhibited her work in the Montreal Museum of Fine Art.

Smily and her husband came to Vancouver in the late 1960s. She has continued to paint portraits, including that

of the family of the Canadian High Commissioner to Hong Kong, and of the retired Archivist of the United States. In addition to works in numerous private and public collections Elizabeth Smily has three of her portraits hanging in the Royal Academy in London, England.

The Art

Julia Askew was the first of seven children born in Chemainus to Thomas George and Isabel Julia Askew. An older brother was born in Victoria two years earlier, but Julia was the first child actually born in the young town of Chemainus. She was delivered on February 22, 1871 at Horse-shoe Bay, with a Native midwife in attendance.

Julia's parents were the builders and owners of the second mill in Chemainus, and Isabel Askew continued to act as resident manager for many years after her husband's death.

Mill Street In 1948

Painted in 1986 , by Mike Svob, B.A., A.F.C.A., Coquitlam, B.C.

6.15M X 13.85M (20' X 45'), MAPLE STREET

The Artist

"As an artist you live a solitary life. Painting here allowed us to share with other artists. There was nothing to sell, no competition, so we could just paint. This was something I really wanted to do."

Mike Svob moved to British Columbia from Welland, Ontario after graduating from the University of Western Ontario and gaining experience in the business world. Art was what everyone told him not to do.

His rendering of Mill Street in 1948 is an impressionistic wave of transparent colour which washes gently over the eye of the viewer much like his watercolours. He is a self-taught painter, who has gained recognition and now exhibits with other well-known members of the Federation of Canadian Artists. Svob has won numerous awards including first prize at the F.C.A. '85 Workshop and the Purchase Award at the 46th Northwest Watercolour Society Show.

The Art

The first building on the left of old Mill Street was used as a Post Office until 1927. That year, street lights made their first appearance in Chemainus, with power provided by the V.L. & M. Company. Beyond the Post Office, towards the water, stood the sawmill superintendant's office.

The mural was totally repainted in 1992.

The company store closed its doors in September, 1949, after 65 years of service. When the building was demolished a year later, wreckers discovered that the frame was made of clear lumber, with some pieces over 40 feet long without a knot or defect of any kind! Several boxes containing cast steel ox shoes, bearing the date 1885, were found under the floor.

Also depicted in the mural is a time clock shelter to the right of the employee parking area. Gordon Wharf and the government wharf recede into the background of Chemainus Harbour.

20

World In Motion

*Painted in 1986 by
Alan Wylie, M.F.A.,
F.C.A., C.S.M.A.,
Crescent Beach
(White Rock), B.C.*

31.08M X 3.69M (101' X 12'), CHEMAINUS ROAD

The Artist
"They showed me this wall that went on forever, and I just had to do it! It was the challenge of the wall!"

Alan Wylie trained as a mural artist in his native Scotland, but few experiences have involved him as much as his painting in Chemainus. *"You're not long in this community before you fall in love with it. I keep turning up like a bad penny."*

Wylie works throughout Canada and the U.S. as a painter and mural artist, but finds time each summer to return to Chemainus, with the excuse that World in Motion isn't quite finished. Melding a number of historic photographs into a cohesive piece of art has been a challenge worthy of Wylie's attention. The resplendence of the mural captures not only the characteristic coastal light, but the joie de vivre, tenacity and spirit of the people as well.

Alan Wylie has lived in Canada since 1967, and has works in many private and public collections in North America and Europe.

The Art
This painting is a montage of historic buildings and events in the area between 1883 and 1939.

On the left are three buildings known as "the Lewisville hotel, store, saloon and barber shop".

Established by former Chemainus teacher Samuel Girdlestone Lewis, this enterprise filled a void when the mill-owned Chemainus Hotel stopped serving liquor. The redesigned 1922 version of the

hotel is depicted behind horse-drawn carriages and an early automobile. To the right in the background are two local businesses of 1892 - A. Howe's Meat Market and Rufus Smith's Blacksmith Shop.

Central to the montage is the Horse-shoe Bay Inn, which stands today. To the right of it appears a facsimile of a document bearing the signatures of two renowned American millionaires who stayed at the hotel in November, 1900 - J.D. Rockefeller (top left), and Andrew Carnegie (bottom left). Mathew Howe, builder and proprietor of the Horseshoe Bay Inn, is portrayed to the right.

A street scene capturing the festivities of the 50th Anniversary Celebration of the Victoria Lumber & Manufacturing Company in 1939 spreads across the right side of the mural.

Chemainus Harbour 1910

Painted in 1987 by Colin Williams, A.R.C.A., Ganges, B.C.

2.1M X 10.5M (7' X 35'), OAK STREET

The Artist

"There is something about painting that is very hard to isolate, to pin down. It is that something extra a photograph doesn't quite catch."

Landscape painter Colin Williams was born and educated in Britain. He was fortunate enough to be in London during the 1960s, an exciting time for innovation in the arts. After receiving the National Diploma in Design from Sunderland College of Art, Williams studied at the Royal College of Art in London and earned the title of Associate of the Royal College (A.R.C.A.) in 1961. He and his family then emigrated to Australia, where he taught at the National School of Art in Sydney for seven years.

In 1969, Williams was invited to the Banff Centre as an artist in residence. It was an opportunity he and his family had been waiting for, and since that time they have called Canada home. Living first in Alberta, his move to Salt Spring Island, B.C. in 1982 has allowed him to work as a full time painter.

While most of Williams' work is in a representational style, he occasionally moves towards the semi-abstract. Most frequently painting in oil, he works in all media, and his subjects tend to be drawn from the rich and varied environment of his west coast surroundings. His paintings are to be found in many public collections internationally, as well as in numerous corporate exhibits.

The Art

In a panoramic view of Chemainus Harbour, this mural captures the colourful memories of the old logging town. Lumber is stacked up along the far hill, waiting to be loaded onto the tall ships and steamers at anchor in the bay. Chemainus Hospital appears on the left.

At the time, the town was a stable community, far past its pioneering stage. The telephone had arrived in 1908. Four churches served the spiritual needs of residents and Chemainus boasted the best baseball team in the region. It was a time of quiet progress after the boom years of mining exploration in the valley.

Lenora Mines At Mt. Sicker

6M X 6.6M (20' X 22'), CORNER OF VICTORIA AND WILLOW STREETS

Painted in 1988 by Peter Bresnen, B.F.A., Halifax, Nova Scotia.

The Artist

"The quality of the art work here in Chemainus is as high as I've ever seen anywhere. We have better murals than are now being painted in Paris!"

Born in Montreal, Peter Bresnen began to paint at the tender age of seven. He pursued studies in Science and Theology before giving in to his obvious talents. He eventually graduated from the Montreal Museum of Fine Arts' School of Art in 1976, was artist in residence at St. Stephen's University in New Brunswick, and then continued his studies toward his B.F.A., which he received in 1981.

He has never strayed far from representational painting, either in his exhibited works or in his murals. He has been painting large tableaux since 1982, with nearly 40 of his murals gracing walls in the Maritimes already. He has held one-man shows in Montreal and in Nova Scotia.

The Art

On May 16, 1897, Harry Smith and a partner staked the famous Lenora claim, named after Smith's only daughter. That began the development of Mt. Sicker as a

copper mining centre. The price of copper was high, and two other companies opened mines in the area.

The town of Mt. Sicker grew to a population of 400, and the community enjoyed such facilities as an interdenominational church, a school, and an opera house. The Lenora mine continued in operation until 1907, when copper prices plummeted and a number of smelters closed down. Less than a year later, the mine's assets were seized by the sheriff. By November of 1908, Mt. Sicker was all but a ghost town. Virtually nothing remains of the townsite today.

It is pictured here in its heyday, when labour was deserting more stable communities like Chemainus for the possibility of a fast fortune in the growing mining industry.

Chemainus Hospital

Painted in 1988 by Doug Driediger, Calgary, Alberta

2.4M X 6M (8' X 20'), CHEMAINUS MEDICAL CLINIC, ESPLANADE STREET

The Artist

"The integrity of the painting has to be a prerequisite to undertaking a commission on this scale. Anything less becomes just another piece of signage."

Armed with an Honours Diploma in Painting from the Alberta College of Art, Calgary native Doug Driediger opened his own graphics business right off the bat. He is an exacting artist who demands that a high degree of intensity and spirit show through in any of his work.

His mural depicting the Chemainus Hospital produced a *"testimonial to a profession dedicated to preserving, enhancing and beginning life",* and is indicative of the painstaking detail which characterizes Driediger's art. In bringing the characters of his mural to life, the people of Chemainus were as important to him as the paints on his palette.

Driediger's paintings are featured in the collections of the Banff Rocky Mountain Resorts and the Thorn Hill Recreation Centre, and appeared in exhibitions associated with the 1988 Winter Olympics in Calgary, Alberta.

The Art

In a composite of scenes, the Chemainus Hospital, built in 1899, sits majestically at the left of the mural. When built, it was the only hospital between Victoria and

CHEMAINUS HOSPITAL. 1904

Nanaimo. It remains a strong focus in the community even today.

Some of the doctors, nurses, staff and patients from over the years are portrayed in the foreground across the expanse of the painting. From left to right are: Nurse Graham, Head Cook Chang, Nurse Johnson, Mrs. Ruth Heslip (wheelchair), Dr. Herbert Burritt Rogers, and Nurse MacDougal, holding an infant.

Dr. Rogers was the first medical doctor to work out of the newly constructed hospital when he began there in 1900. Before obtaining his medical degree from McGill University in Montreal, he had the distinction of being one of Canada's earliest appendectomy patients. While working as a postal inspector, he again led the way, carrying the first official mail to Victoria on the newly completed Canadian Pacific Railway. He was a well-loved resident of Chemainus for many years and retired as the Medical Superintendant of the Chemainus Hospital in 1936.

Second Chemainus Sawmill

Painted in 1988 by Bruce Rickett, Dartmouth, Nova Scotia.

2.4M X 6M (8' X 20'), *CHEMAINUS ROAD*

The Artist

"I don't look at this as a mural. I see it only as a larger painting, and so I approach it with the same intensity and spirit as I would any of my paintings. The artistic value is the prime ingredient of my work."

As a first time mural artist, Bruce Rickett carried with him to Chemainus a newness and intensity which shone through in his painting of Second Chemainus Sawmill. He was able to establish a strong relationship with the place and the subject he worked with.

Rickett was born in Malawi, Central Africa, studied art at the City and Guilds of London Art School in England, and then came to Canada. He earned a B.F.A. degree at the Nova Scotia College of Art and Design before achieving a post graduate art history degree at the University of Illinois.

As well as curatorial experience for galleries and exhibits, Rickett has been building a body of work over the last number of years. He has found a home in Dartmouth, Nova Scotia, and continues to be a prolific painter.

The Art

This sawmill was the second to be built on the same site. Constructed in 1879 by T.G. Askew, it was converted to steam power by Croft and Severne in 1883. The mural is based on a photograph in 1886.

A mill operated continuously at this site for over 100 years before shutting down for a short period in 1983. In 1985, MacMillan Bloedel opened a new modern equipped mill which marks the site of the longest continuous lumber production in all of British Columbia.

(25)

Waiting For The Whistle

Painted in 1989 by Robert Dafford, Lafayette, Louisiana.

36.58M X 3.05M (120' X 10'), CYPRESS STREET

The Artist
One of America's most prominent mural artists, Robert Dafford considers his artistic career began as early as high school. His studies in art at the University of Southwestern Louisiana were interrupted by the Viet Nam war, and he served for three years as a naval illustrator and draftsman aboard the U.S.S. Independence in the Mediterranean. Since then, he has painted more than fifty

murals, ten of which are in Canada. Most recently, Dafford has worked in Europe and the central U.S., but he always returns home to Louisiana where he resides with his partner and wife and their two daughters.

Brother and fellow artist Douglas Dafford assisted with Waiting for the Whistle. The two artists often collaborate, Douglas handling the engineering challenges while Robert concentrates on the artistic aspects of a project.

The Art
On a quiet Saturday afternoon in November 1923, a massive and violent fire consumed the entire roof of the third

Chemainus mill and the structure collapsed. In the spring of 1924, much to the relief of the townspeople, the foundations were laid for a new mill, to be known as one of the largest of its kind in the world. It was not until 1940, however, that a new whistle was installed on the roof of the fourth mill.

The central theme of this expansive tryptic is that of the mill and its workers anticipating the end of the shift with the sounding of the handsomely crafted steam-operated whistle. Sombre greens and blues mark the dying light of an evening in summer.

To the left is an image of Bob Swanson, mill engineer and the inventor of the

whistle, standing beside the gleaming brass and piping of the device itself. This is superimposed on a sepia-like composition of mill workers who have just completed the rebuilding of the interlocking skidder. Jack Work (with hat), inspector for the E&N Railway, gave the okay for the machine to be returned to the tracks. Swanson was responsible for the refitting, devising air controls and a second boiler for extra power.

To the right is another portrait of mill workers assembling and installing the new mill whistle in 1940, set against a sepia-like reproduction of the mill's bull saw. During its heyday, the fourth mill was an example of efficiency and productivity, and was renowned for its size and modernity. The whistle was retired with the mill in the early 1980's, and is now on display in the Chemainus Valley Museum.

26

Chemainus - The War Years - Circa 1915

Painted in 1989 by Susan Tooke Crichton, Halifax, Nova Scotia

10.65M X 2.13M (35' X 7'), MAPLE STREET

The Artist
"I paint on a fairly large scale. I felt that this would be really challenging, and it was. I don't like to turn down challenges."

Chemainus, The War Years was Susan Tooke Crichton's first mural project. A lot of research went into determining the fine detail evident in the final wall painting, down to the correct insignia on the uniforms and the varied dress of the civilians on the railway platform. This detail is the signature of Chrichton's work.

In 1980, Crichton immigrated to Canada from the Eastern United States. She had taken a Bachelor of Fine Arts at Virginia Commonwealth University, had done graduate work in Media Studies at the New School for Social Research in New York City and had taught art in New Jersey for eight years prior to leaving her native country.

Crichton has now established herself as an artist in Halifax, Nova Scotia, painting predominantly in acrylics. A typical work, strongly grounded in realism and minutely detailed, will take her perhaps four months to complete. In recognition of her skill and attention to detail, she was chosen by the Nova Scotia Art Gallery to exhibit her work in a first province-wide survey of contemporary art. Other murals now figure in her body of work, and she continues to paint on a smaller scale as well.

The Art

Patriotic feelings ran high as many men from Chemainus and area scrambled to join up soon after war was declared. By the end of September 1914 the mill had closed due to the war's impact on shipping, convincing many more volunteers to enlist.

A reserved excitement, mixed with apprehension and a certain sadness, marks the faces of the young soldiers arrested in time in this grouping. They are members of the 67th Battalion out of Victoria, awaiting the train which for many would mark the last journey they would make from this community.

Their connection to the land they had laboured so hard to tame was severed. They left behind the fields and forests, the homesteads and the growing village, the families and elders who would have to carry on. By the end of 1915, more than fifteen percent of the local population had gone off to this bloody war, a significant number never to return.

MURAL REFERENCE NUMBER 27

The Spirit Of Chemainus

Painted in 1991 by Dan Sawatzky assisted by Peter Sawatzky

4.57M X 4.57M (15' X 15'), LAUREL STREET

The Artist

As the youngest mural artist to participate in bringing the history of Chemainus to life, Peter Sawatzky was just fifteen when he assisted on his first mural in 1991. He has shown a keen interest in many media, especially painting and sculpture. Because of his special talents and dedication to art, Sawatzky helped to create for himself a unique course of studies in three-dimensional design for his last two years of high school.

Sawatzky looks forward to making art a career, and is well on his way to doing so. He has assisted his father on mural projects all over Canada and the United States, and has travelled to Europe and Japan to study and appreciate art and culture. He resides in Chemainus with his family, and anticipates further art education as well as plenty of practical experience following his graduation from high school.

The Art

Hints of a pristine coastline, heavily treed and dripping green, peep out from behind a glimmering impressionistic image of the brigantine Spirit of Chemainus. The suggestion of activity on the deck, with five faceless figures, symbolizes an earlier time when such vessels were commonly seen in Chemainus Bay, and indeed all along the coast of British Columbia.

This sailing ship was built and launched in Chemainus in 1985 as an offshoot of, and a tribute to, the original Chemainus Festival of Murals. Constructed by master shipwrights, the fine lines and textured surfaces of the boat are captured in the muted colours of the painting. Spirit of Chemainus may oft be seen plying the waters of Georgia Strait and the Gulf Islands.

NO.3
Climax Engine

Painted in 1991 by Dan Sawatzky, Chemainus, B.C.

4.57M X 4.42M (15' X 14'6"), ALDER STREET

The Artist
"Design and fabrication of outrageous things is what I do. Murals are just a part of that now, albeit a big part."

Dan Sawatzky first painted a mural in Chemainus as a visiting artist in 1983. Mural painting has become a way of life for not only Dan, but his entire family. More than forty murals later, all family members are involved, and all help in the family business - called "Sawatzky's Imagination Corporation."

Sawatzky's artistic roots working in pen and ink still show in some of the detail of his larger projects. Murals have become so much a part of Sawatzky's life that he is now one of a handful of artists in North America presently making a living as a full-time mural painter. He works at a fever pace, and attacks any project with an energy akin to a white tornado. In 1991, he painted fourteen murals in North America and Japan.

As his skill and style evolve, Sawatzky's paintings grow more evocative, using more colour and light, rather than intricate detail to suggest mood and locale. His reputation is now taking him into three-dimensional work, and he is involved in theme parks in B.C. and elsewhere in North America.

The Art

A huge, foreshortened iron horse steams and belches dark smoke as it leaps out of its frame and almost off the wall of artist Dan Sawatzky's home and studio. The subject, a working engine operating in the Chemainus area early this century, is of particular interest to the artist, who has always been fascinated by trains.

Engineer Sam Alexander operated the

No. 3 Climax Engine as it hauled logs along the rails of the Chemainus Valley. The E&N Railway was completed in 1886, although working trains had been a familiar sight in the community for some years already. The larger engines plied the rails through the hills and valleys of the E&N land belt, from which the Victoria Lumber and Manufacturing Company drew a great deal of its timber. Smaller, more compact engines worked nearer to and at the mill, shunting timber and finished products to where they were needed.

The Winning Float

29

Painted in 1991 by Joyce H. Kamikura, Richmond, B.C.

9.45M X3.35M (31' X 11'), CROFT STREET

The Artist

"What attracted me was the freedom to design the mural based on the subject. I could visualize all those colours! It was a part of my history, of my parents' history."

Born in Steveston and raised in Japan, Joyce Kamikura came late to life as an artist. When she returned to Canada in 1956, she studied to obtain a degree in Commerce and Business Administration. Only in 1982 did she return to college to formally study art. She has since worked as a full-time artist.

The painting of The Winning Float was a challenge in which Kamikura wished to achieve a sense of the ethereal light and transparency of watercolour, as well as capturing the richness of the pigments found in traditional Japanese fabrics.

Kamikura works in watercolour and mixed media, and has developed a style recognizable for its jewel-like colours and sense of movement. The artist has achieved recognition in many exhibitions in Canada and internationally. Her works may be found in collections as far afield as England and Japan.

The Art

The date was June 30, 1939 - the Golden Jubilee of the Victoria Lumber and Manufacturing Company, the lifeblood of

The Winning Float
Joyce H. Kamikura
©1991

the modern town of Chemainus. The summer breeze rustled leaves and pulled at the lengths of the swaying silk kimonos worn by members of the Japanese Canadian community. Theirs was the winning float in a record-breaking parade which stretched over three-quarters of a mile (1km) and began two days of festivities.

In stark contrast to the gentle dance of the women's clothing are the sturdy siennas and rusts of an expanse of forest and rock across the bay, the eternal backdrop to all activity in the town. Japanese culture likewise survived side by side the picket fence propriety of a dominant society which became increasingly intolerant of differences as war loomed. By 1942, there was not a single Japanese Canadian resident in the town - all had been forcibly moved to internment camps.

In the summer of 1991, special efforts were undertaken to commemorate the rich and valuable contribution of Japanese Canadians to the community of Chemainus. The Winning Float is a result of those efforts, and pays tribute to citizens who so long ago took such joy in celebrating the history of the town.

The Lone Scout

Painted in 1991 by Stanley Hiromichi Taniwa, Clanwilliam, Manitoba

6.10M X 2.59M (20' X 8'6"), CROFT STREET

The Artist

"I went back to Chemainus somehow looking for my home. When they showed me the photos, there was my father, there were my uncles! Shige, I found out, was a good friend of my dad's. Painting the mural was a really personal statement."

Stan Taniwa left Chemainus as a baby,

evacuated with his parents and six siblings to an internment camp in the interior of B.C. during WWII. What followed was an extremely difficult time for Japanese Canadians. Taniwa's father died, leaving a large family for his mother to raise single-handedly. The Taniwas settled in Thunder Bay, Ontario, where Stan originally studied architectural drafting.

When he undertook fine art studies at the University of Manitoba, it was to pursue an interest in ceramics. He began exhibiting his work in 1970, and has since shown his ceramic creations from Ontario to Alberta. Taniwa teaches and is a juror for the Canada Council and the Manitoba Festival of the Arts. He has restored an old brick church in Eden, Manitoba, where he has established his home and studio. Since The Lone Scout was painted in 1991, Taniwa has completed other paintings as well as continuing his work in clay.

The Art

Edward Shige Yoshida was born in Victoria, B.C. in 1908, and was raised in the quiet mill town of Chemainus. In 1929, he realized his dream in starting the 2nd Chemainus Boy Scouts, an all-Japanese Canadian troop and the first of its kind in the country. The delicate, porcelain plate quality of his portrait in the mural The Lone Scout belies the wit, energy and

determination of this slightly-built but significant character in the life of Chemainus.

Chemainus town was home to a community of 300 Japanese Canadians who had settled in the area between 1900 and the 1940s. Mill workers, fishers, and business people and their families, all were

interned after the attack on Pearl Harbour in the U.S. precipitated an attitude of paranoia and mistrust towards Canadians of Japanese descent.

By a series of coincidences, Stan Taniwa

came to paint The Lone Scout, and included in the black and white gathering in the background of the mural are members of his family, then and now. The location of Taniwa's family home is just across the street from his mural.

31

The Lumber Barons

Painted in 1992 by Constance Greig-Manning, assisted by Bill Manning, Kenilworth, Ontario

9.75M X 4.88M (32' X 16'), MILL STREET

The Artist

"People who watch art being created find it less threatening. They feel they are part of the process, instead of the art being something apart, something they don't understand."

As an artist used to working big (many of her canvases are nearly mural size),

Constance Greig-Manning was thrilled by her first mural experience. Working out in the open air, collaborating with her husband as her assistant and meeting and talking with innumerable passers-by opened a new and exciting artistic realm for her.

Constance now lives and works here in Chemainus, with husband and artist, Bill Manning. She has been painting since she was a child, and was encouraged to become an artist in high school. She followed up with studies in experimental art at the University of Calgary.

Since then, Greig-Manning has moved back towards a more traditional artistic style, and is recognized for her expertise in portraiture. The challenge for her in the Lumber Barons, was *"to find a balance between two very strong personalities, and a number of two and three-dimensional elements on a wall interrupted by three windows and a door!"*

The Art

The deep blues and purples of the sea and mountains on the left flank the solemn portrait of Mill Manager John Humbird, who in 1924 oversaw the building of the fourth Chemainus mill, one of the largest of its kind in the world. The mural symbolizes the rivalry and relationship between Humbird and another powerful character in Chemainus history, H.R. MacMillan. The lumber baron, whose company in the early 1940's purchased the huge fourth mill pictured in the mural,

appears at the centre of the painting.

    After the takeover of the mill, the word "Manufacturing" was dropped from the name, and it became simply the Victoria Lumber Co.. The closed door below MacMillan represents the mill office door, behind which took place much of the history of the mill's success over the years. The mural is bordered on the right by images of both the wealth of the natural forest and the richness of its harvest, the wood products which made many fortunes.

The Telephone Company - Circa 1915

Painted in 1992 by Cim MacDonald, A.F.C.A., N.W.W.S., Chemainus, B.C.

3.66M X 3.05M (12' X 10'), WILLOW STREET

The Artist

Born in Scotland, Cim MacDonald came with her family to Victoria when she was seven. She completed her schooling with a major in art. After working for the Provincial Government in Victoria, she took a job in Crofton, where she spent the better part of the past twenty years.

MacDonald remembers painting greenware in post-war Scotland, sitting around the kitchen table with her mother, aunts and grandmother. When her father joined a seniors art class, he inspired Cim to try her hand at painting again. A number of courses later, she began to exhibit her art and to teach others to paint. Recently, she hosted a beginner course in watercolour for television.

Because of her long affiliation with the

lumber industry, MacDonald is known for her commissions of industrial and marine themes. Her paintings can be found in corporate collections including Rivtow, and Fletcher Challenge Canada. IBM and Domtar have included her work in their Canada-wide exhibitions. MacDonald exhibits her work in Duncan and in Toronto. She lives just south of Chemainus where she and her husband are restoring an old farmhouse.

The Art

The telephone appeared in Chemainus in 1908. The first telephone company offices were located in a private house on Maple Street but moved seven years later to larger premises. The Victorian residence pictured here served as the telephone exchange for thirty telephones in the community, and was home to Daisy Bonde, pictured on the left. Daisy ran the exchange as a supervisor. Standing at her side is Sophia Horton (Syme), the first paid operator to work at

the exchange.

From across Willow Street, the viewers feel they have stepped back in time. Two serious young women in laced boots and

long skirts wait to greet them on the Victorian porch. A client's bicycle leans against the weathered clapboard veranda. The picket fence, with its gate wide and welcoming, surrounds flower boxes. A real, old-fashioned boardwalk and stairs

beckon the visitor to step up for a chat.

The whole effect is a personal, scaled-down, life-like depiction of a typical Chemainus street scene back in simpler times, when demand required that telephone service be offered during daylight hours only.

33

Memories of A Chinese Boy

Painted in 1996 by Cheng Shu-Ren (Arthur), Surrey, B.C.

5M X 10M (16'8" X 33'4"), CHEMAINUS ROAD

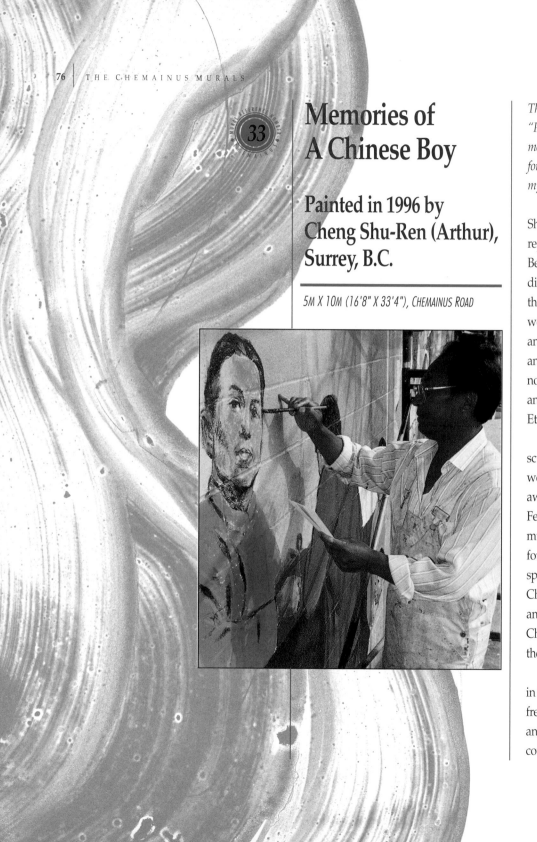

The Artist
"Painting the mural in Chemainus, this most important mural city, is an honour for me. It is what I am most proud of in my artistic life in Canada."

Born in Nanchang, China, Cheng Shu-Ren (Arthur Cheng) established his reputation as an outstanding artist in Beijing. He has won many awards with distinction and in 1985, he was named in the British Who's Who. His versatile works include extensive garden and park designs in Shanghai, and he has graced Surrey, B.C., now his home, with his design and construction of the "Chinese Eternal Garden."

His bronze and marble sculptures and monuments have won for him many prestigious awards from the Shanghai Arts Festival. His submission for this mural was chosen from among fourteen in a competition sponsored by the Canadian Chinese Artist Federation, and he became the first Chinese artist to enhance the walls of Chemainus.

Arthur came to Canada in 1990 and now enjoys the freedom of artistic experiences and the new challenges this country offers.

His daughter, Cheng Ying, assisted him in painting Memories of a Chinese Boy, which they completed in just fourteen days.

The Art
Many newcomers from China worked in the mines at Mt. Sicker. Among them was Shong Hai Chang, who opened a general store before the turn of the century. He called it "Sam Yick Kee"

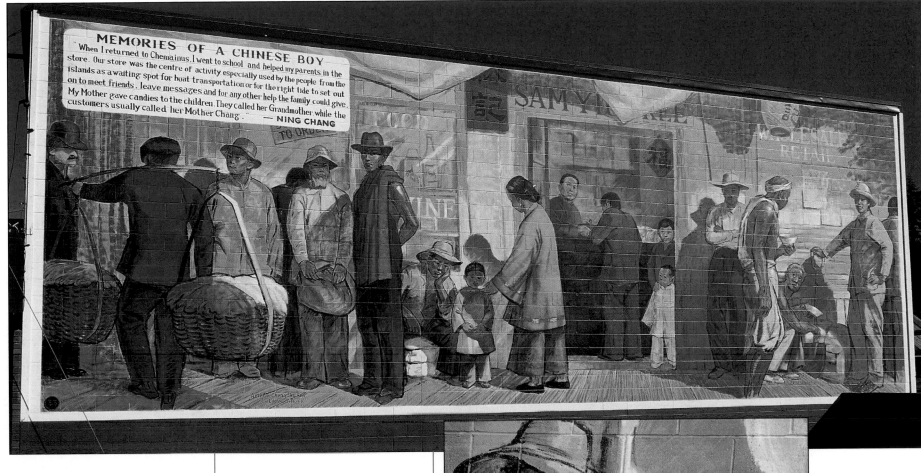

MEMORIES OF A CHINESE BOY

"When I returned to Chemainus, I went to school and helped my parents in the store. Our store was the centre of activity especially used by the people from the islands as a waiting spot for boat transportation or for the right tide to set out on to meet friends, leave messages and for any other help the family could give. My Mother gave candies to the children. They called her Grandmother while the customers usually called her Mother Chang." — **NING CHANG**

meaning "three benefits". The mural portrays the store operated by his son, Ning Chang, who was the first Chinese Child born in Chemainus (1913). The street scene illustrates this popular meeting place and focal point for Chinese immigrants. This waterfront store supplied the community with commodities and foods imported directly from China. The Changs also operated a piggery and sold dressed hogs to local meat markets. Shong Hai Chang's passing in 1934 was marked by the largest Chinese funeral ever to take place in Chemainus. His son, Ning Chang, took over the business located on Oak Street at the site of the now 49th Parallel Grocery store. His descendants still reside in Chemainus.

A Day In The Life Of Chemainus

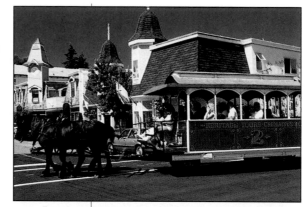

(Counterclockwise from top)

Carriage tours of Chemainus

Jazz in the park

Teddy Bears' Picnic

The old fashioned joys of ice cream

Pancake breakfast

Concert in Heritage Square

Heritage Square

This project was one of the most challenging faced by the Festival of Murals.

Conceived and spearheaded by Karl Schutz, it began in 1983 with the construction of the Heritage Wall. It didn't take long to realize that the adjacent land, originally slated to be a parking lot, would be better utilized instead to create a park for all people.

Mural artist Dan Sawatzky designed and oversaw the construction of Heritage Square. Over a period of three years, hundreds of volunteer hours and funding through grants and donations from dozens of individuals saw the project through to completion.

Heritage Square is now a tranquil setting ideal for meeting friends or just resting. It is centrally located on the corner of Chemainus Road and Mill Street. A stop here can be a perfect jumping off point for a walking tour of the murals, or it can be the quiet spot at which to end a tour and contemplate the artistry of both human and natural forces.

Spool Donkey

Designed and carved in 1983 by Elmar Schultes

The Artist

"Carving was something I always wanted to do."

At the age of 15, Elmar Schultes left his German home to apprentice as a chef. He became proficient as a culinary sculptor during 20 years in the hotel business.

In 1960, he came to Vancouver to live, and filled the prestigious position of executive chef at Trader Vic's (Bayshore Hotel). There, he was commissioned to carve 18 large cedar figures for the company's restaurants in Canada and the United States.

Schultes' popular red cedar and fine figures (some of which have been purchased for members of visiting Trade Commissions) demonstrate both the artist's sensitivity and a liveliness in the characters he carves.

The Art

Carved in the shadow of the historic Chemainus waterwheel, this monumental sculpture now welcomes visitors to the centre of town.

The carving is based on the first mural to be painted in Chemainus, Frank Lewis' Steam Donkey At Work. The three-dimensional cedar depiction shows the Dolbeer steam donkey, built in San Francisco in 1882. The engine was a concave drum on which the cable, held by the well-gloved hands of the "spool-tender", was wound, thus drawing the log from the woods. The cable was then retracted by a "horse-line".

The Little Town That Did©
CHEMAINUS
MUNICIPALITY OF NORTH COWICHAN

In Search Of Snipes

Designed and cast in 1986 by Glenn Spicer, Maple Bay, B.C.

The Artist

"When I was making the figures for the sculpture in Heritage Square, I would walk into my studio and they would give me a start! I'd think someone was in my studio".

Born and raised in Ontario, Glenn Spicer received a B.Sc. from the University of Guelph. For a while he put both his science background and his artistic abilities to work as a paleontology display artist sculpting dinosaur skulls with the Royal Ontario Museum and as a scientific illustrator for the Botany Department of the University of Guelph.

After his move to the West Coast, Glenn became a layout artist with the Vancouver Folk Music Festival, and gained experience as a research assistant and media lab manager with the Department of Communications Media and Technology, Faculty of Education, U.B.C. His growing love of things artistic led him to complete three years at the Emily Carr College of Art and Design in Vancouver.

Spicer has since worked as a senior display artist for the Vancouver Aquarium, and now freelances as a sculptor and stained glass artist.

The Art

On a moonlit summer's night in 1913, two strangers found their way into Chemainus. While socializing with the locals, they were told of elusive snipes hiding in the forest, and that this would be a perfect night to catch them. The strangers were shown the secret place in the woods and instructed to hold a lit lantern in front of an open sack, into which the locals, acting as beaters, would drive the snipe.

The townsfolk then stole back to the village. After hours of waiting, the boys realized they had been innocent victims of a bit of mischief, and they too returned to the town to join the others and share in a good laugh.

Snipes, like dreams, can be captured. Through hard work, Chemainus embraced its "snipes" when yesterday's dreams became today's realities.

Spirit of the Earth

(work in progress)

Designed and carved by Daniel Cline, Chemainus, B.C.

Assisted by Ted Speirs and Marcus Carter

11' X 3' X 3', *LOCATION TO BE FINALIZED*

The Artist

"Inwardly, in contemplation, I reflect upon the nature of humankind, our spiritual journey, our interconnectedness with all things, and these thoughts and ideas find expression in much of my work."

Born in St. Catherines, Ontario, Daniel's interest in sculpture began at an early age, creating figures of fantasy in clay. Primarily self-taught, he uses a variety of materials including Vancouver Island marble, exotic alabasters of the southwest, and Brazilian and African soapstone. Having moved to Vancouver Island in 1990, Daniel is continually made aware of the beauty of the natural world; whales, dolphins, bears, eagles, and fish are often the subjects of his sculpture, expressing his respect for the wonders of creation.

The Art

"The process of time travel, from primeval sea bed, to the hand and spirit of a creative being is a difficult and long one. To wrestle an image from an ancient rock, to reveal a dream in stone, is a sculptor's passion."

The marble sculpture represents a mystic native princess, her robe adorned with the wildlife of Vancouver Island. An Orca dives from her hair, an Eagle soars interconnected with a Salmon leaping upwards. The upper half of the sculpture depicts the quiet calm of the earth, while the lower portion depicts the world in action. The Princess represents the Earth, the lifegiver, the source of our livelihood. She is stone – marble, transcending thousands of years of pressure and heat, to be transformed again.

More Sculptures of Chemainus

Private Commissions for Public Enjoyment

(Clockwise from top left)

SEA CAPTAIN
by Glenn Spicer, Willow Street

CHARLIE ABBOT - THE HERMIT
by Glenn Spicer,
Pacific Rim Artisan Village

THREE GENERATIONS
by Sandy Clark, Legion Street

THE WATER WHEEL
Replica of water wheel from
original, Water Wheel Park

History And Art Hand In Hand With Business

The economic spin-offs from the Chemainus Murals have been phenomenal. Major tour operators clamour to stop here on their rounds of picturesque Vancouver Island. Publications worldwide have described the mural art and the atmosphere of the town in glowing terms, attracting tourists from every continent.

But more importantly, businesses, which are strong and healthy employers for the area, have opened their doors in record numbers. Over one hundred new businesses have successfully established themselves in Chemainus since the mural project began in 1982. Confidence and initiative by both established and new merchants has come as part and parcel of the town's rejuvenation.

The growing number of new enterprises that have opened for business in Chemainus include galleries, studios and workshops for items as diverse as fabric arts, painting, sculpture, gem cutting, glass blowing, graphic design and photography. Toy making is alive and well. Also, many new charming Bed & Breakfasts have opened, each offering unique accommodation and cuisine. Antiques are becoming a dominant theme in Chemainus, along with cafes, bakeries and original gift shops. Outlets for creative artistry in the kitchen and other parts of the family home have added to the quality and diversity of the commercial areas.

Volunteers are our Strength

Since the mural project began in 1982, volunteer participation has been central to its success. Over a hundred volunteers from the region donate their time each season, from mid-May through late September to staff the mural information kiosk in the town's centre. From morning to evening, these committed citizens offer information to visitors, detailing the history behind the murals and the town, and selling official Festival of Murals souvenirs.

Without volunteers, the Festival of Murals would never have happened. Volunteers were instrumental in setting the stage for the first murals to be painted. They constructed Heritage Square and the path to Old Town. They continue to offer their time for numerous functions related to the mural project on a regular basis.

Over the years, this generosity has resulted in the donation of some $400,000 worth of person/hours to the success of the Chemainus Festival of Murals. Their amazing contribution was officially recognized by the government of British Columbia in early 1989.

The Chemainus Festival of Murals Society extends a heartfelt thanks for the dedication of all the volunteers who really make Chemainus "The Little Town That Did"©.

MURAL SPONSORS

COMMUNICATIONS CANADA
CULTURAL INITIATIVES
PROGRAM
◆
B.C. TEL
◆
MUNICIPALITY OF
NORTH COWICHAN
◆
CHEMAINUS
MEDICAL COMMUNITY
◆
CHEMAINUS VALLEY
HISTORICAL SOCIETY
◆
CIBC
◆
JAPANESE CANADIAN
REDRESS FOUNDATION
◆
MACMILLAN BLOEDEL
◆
PACIFIC SHORES INN
◆
ROBINSON, LITTLE &
COMPANY, LIMITED
◆
DAN SAWATZKY
◆
THE MACMILLAN FOUNDATION
MRS. JEAN SOUTHAM
◆
CHINESE CANADIAN
ARTISTS FEDERATION
Professor Johnson S. Chow,
Mr. Gary Ho, Mrs. Alice Shen
◆
THE FESTIVAL OF MURALS SOCIETY
DENISE SHARIATMADARI
◆ ◆ ◆ ◆

Our Sponsors...

We of the Chemainus Festival of Murals Society would like to thank the many sponsors and granting agencies who made this imaginative project possible.

Their considerable financial support created a permanent work of vision, one that will certainly make its mark on the future. We salute you!

Grants

Communications Canada –
Cultural Incentives Program
Employment and
Immigration Canada
Canada Employment –
Summer Program
Canada Works
Employment Grant
Challenge 86 Student
Employment Program
Municipality of
North Cowichan
Ministry of Tourism,
Recreation & Culture
B.C. Lottery
Ministry of Municipal Affairs,
Downtown Revitalization
Ministry of Social Services
and Housing
Ministry of Labour
Employment Grant
Vancouver Foundation

Corporate and Private Donations & Donations in-Kind

Words Can Never Express...

adequately the debt of gratitude owed to the many businesses and individuals who have generously donated their time, skills, money and materials to create the vibrant artistic community and thriving centre of hospitality which is Chemainus today. After sixteen years since the project began, the number of individuals and businesses whose names deserve inclusion here would fill several pages – a tribute to the extent of the community's involvement.

The murals, like gift wrap on the galleries, restaurants, and shops, both new and old, will stand as witness to the indomitable spirit of the people of this valley. Visitors from around the world will be heartened by the story told on the walls of Chemainus, and by the warmth of the welcome from those whose story it is.

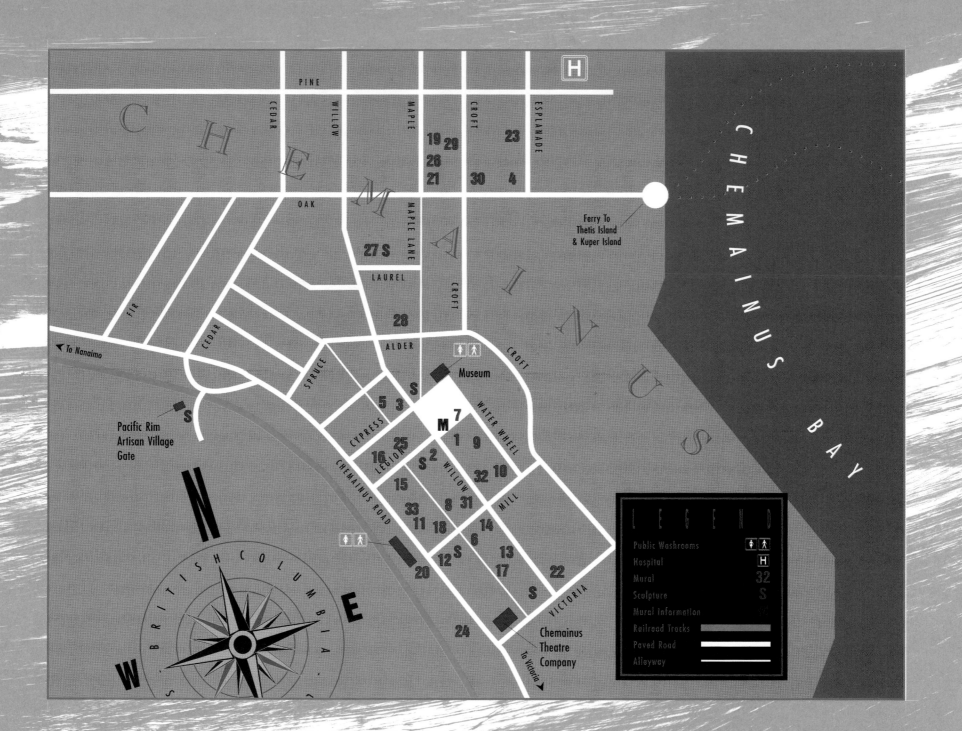

PINE

CEDAR

WILLOW

MAPLE

CROFT

ESPLANADE

CHEMAINUS

H

CHEMAINUS BAY

19 29
26
21

23
30   4

OAK

MAPLE LANE

Ferry To
Thetis Island
& Kuper Island

27 S

CROFT

LAUREL

28

To Nanaimo

ALDER

CROFT

FIR

CEDAR

SPRUCE

Museum

5 3

S

Pacific Rim
Artisan Village
Gate

S

WATER WHEEL

M 7

CYPRESS

25

1   9

LEGION

16

S 2

WILLOW

32 10

N

15

MILL

BRITISH COLUMBIA

CHEMAINUS ROAD

33
11   18

8 31

14

6

12 S

13
17

22

E

20

S

VICTORIA

W

S

24

Chemainus
Theatre
Company

To Victoria

LEGEND

Public Washrooms

Hospital   H

Mural   32

Sculpture   S

Mural Information

Railroad Tracks

Paved Road

Alleyway

The *Chemainus* MURALS

Festival of Murals

SINCE 1985

MURAL LOCATION GUIDE

A Mural Reference Number corresponds to a particular mural. Look for these numbers on each mural. Refer to numbers for location on the map.

VANCOUVER

NANAIMO

CHEMAINUS

VICTORIA

SEATTLE

Discover
NORTH COWICHAN

Home to Chemainus, Crofton, Maple Bay and Genoa Bay

Celebrating
125 Years
1873 – 1998